Lien G

A Journal of Cornish Folklore

Number 3

Compiled and edited by

Alex Langstone

Spirit of Albion Books

in association with

Cornish Folklore
Lien Gwerin a Gernow
www.cornishfolklore.co.uk

This collection published in 2019 by

Spirit of Albion Books, Cornwall, UK

www.spiritofalbionbooks.co.uk

in association with

Cornish Folklore ~ Lien Gwerin a Gernow

www.cornishfolklore.co.uk

ISBN 978-0-9563554-7-8

ISSN 2515-2483

With grateful thanks to:

Paul Atlas-Saunders, Merv Davey, Alan M. Kent,
Sheridan James Lunt, Andy Norfolk and Craig Weatherhill

Contents

Illustrations

Paul Atlas-Saunders, page 4, 12, 16, 18, 49. H. A. Simcoe, page 17. William Hawkins, page 19. Seaton Mermaid, page 25 (by C S?) Sheridan James Lunt, page 38, 40
J. T. Blight, page 65.

All photographs by Alex Langstone

Cover Art

Front cover ~ from the *Old Looe Stories and Legends* set of cards: '*The Seaton Mermaid*' (1937). Artist unknown, but with the initials C S or S C.
Back cover ~ 'Ghost Ship of Porthcurno' by
Paul Atlas-Saunders

The Pencarrow Hunt

Merv Davey

Folklore and tradition travel through the landscape and through time bearing the stories, memories, and ideas of a community. Indeed the very term "Folk" was coined by the German philosopher Johann Herder who saw these traditions as representing the very soul of the people.[1] There is a beautiful paradox here in that whilst folk tradition represents continuity with the deep past, the way that it is mediated and explained also tells the story of the people providing that explanation at a given moment in time. The story of "The Pencarrow Hunt" provides a fascinating illustration of this.

"Pencarrow Hunt" as the song is known in North Cornwall becomes "Lord Arscott of Tetcott" along the Cornwall Devon border and shares its melody with a Welsh song called "Difyrwch Gwyr Dyfi" (Delight of the men of Dovey). The narrative focuses on Pencarrow House, near Bodmin, and a bucolic fox hunt across the moors with Lord John Arscott whose family owned much of the land between

---

[1] Johann Gottfried Von Herder, ed. Volkslieder. (Leipzig, Weygandschen Buchhandlung,1778: but see discussion of this in John Francmanis, "Folk song and the 'folk': a relationship illuminated by Frank Kidson's Traditional Tunes" in Folk Song: Tradition, Revival, and Re-Creation, ed. Ian Russel and David Atkinson (Aberdeen, The Elphinstone Institute, 2004), p186-187.

here and Tetcott just over the border. The chase takes us to the towering cliffs of North Cornwall where it sometimes ends with the demise of the fox; and sometimes ends with the hounds leaping off the cliffs to meet their doom on the rocks below closely followed by Lord Arscott and friends.

In good folkloric style the hunters reappear in ghostly form from time to time and we also meet the mysterious Black John. Black John was Lord Arscott's servant who played the role of court jester to entertain his guests. One of his tricks was to swallow and regurgitate a live mouse on a string! Black John lived and ran with the hounds so that he was first in on the kill at the end of the hunt.[2] The date of "fifty two" in the lyrics is variously interpreted as 1652 when there was a Lord John Arscott but no record of a Black John: 1752 when there was a candidate for Black John but the Lord was an Arthur Arscott and not John; and 1772 when there was again a Lord John Arscott who was the last of his line.[3] It is very easy to go down the metaphoric rabbit hole here and look for historic hereditary facts which have little to do with the folklore.

There was once a view that committing the narrative or melody of a folk song to print was to fix it forever and stop the process of change in oral tradition. In practice, quite the opposite is often the case and appearance in print serves to encourage the process of evolution and change. This certainly seems to be what happened to "The Pencarrow Hunt". We get an early glimpse of the lyrics and the story in the form a poem submitted to a "gentleman's" periodical called Willis's Current

---

[2] Robert Stephen Hawker. Footprints of Former Men in Far Cornwall. (London, 1870)

[3] http://landedfamilies.blogspot.com/2015/10/188-arscotsland.htmlt-of-tetcott-and-dun

Notes by the redoubtable Rev Robert Stephen Hawker in 1853:[4]

On the ninth of November, in the year Fifty-Two,
Three jolly foxhunters. All sons of the blue;
They rode from Pencarrow, not fearing a wet coat,
To take their diversion with Arscott of Tetcott.

He went to his kennel an took them within;
"On Monday" said Arscott, "our joys shall begin;
Both horse and hounds, how they pant to be gone,
How they'll follow 'foot, not forgetting Black John".

When Monday was come, right early at morn,
John Arscott arose, and he took down his horn;
He gave it a flourish so loud in the hall,
Each heard the glad summons and came at the call.

They heard it with pleasure, but Webb was first dress'd,
Resolving to give a cold pig to the rest;
Bold Bob and the Briton, they hasten'd down the stairs,
'Twas generally supposed they neglected their pray'rs.

At breakfast they scrambled for butter and toast,
But Webb was impatient that time should be lost;
So old Cheyney was ordered to bring to the door,
Both horses and hounds, and away to the moor.

---

[4] Robert Stephen Hawker. "Ballad Lore" in Willis, G. Current Notes: a series of articles on Antiquities, Biography Heraldry, History. Language. Literature. Topography curious customs &c. (London, G. Willis, 1853)

"On Monday", said Arscott, as he mounted his nag,
"I look to old Blackcap, for he'll hit the drag!"
The drag it was hit, they said it was old,
For drag in the morning could not be so cold.

They prick'd it along, to Becket and Thorn
And here the old dogs they set out, I'll be sworn,
'Twas Ringwood and Rally, with capital scent,
Bold Princess and Madcap, Good God! How they went!

How far did they make it? How far went they on?
How far did they make it"? said Simon the Son;
"O'er the moors" said Joe Goodman, "Hark to the Bacchus,
the word!"
"Hark to Vulcan" Cried Arscott "that's it, by the Lord!"

"Hark to princess!" says Arscott; "there's a fresh Tally-ho!"
The dogs they soon caught it, and how they did go!
"Twas Princess and Madcap, and Ringwood and Ralley,
They charmed every hill and they echoed each valley.

From Becket, through Thorn, they went on their way,
To Swannacott Wood without break or delay
And when they came there, how they sounded again!
"What music it is!" cried the glad Whitestone Men.

In haste came up Arscott – "Oh, where are they gone?"
"They are off to the cliffs," then said Simon the son;
Through Wike, and through Poundstock, St Gennys
They went.
And when Reynard came there, he gave up by consent.

So, when Reynard was dead, we broke up the field,
With joy in our hearts that we made him to yield;
And when he came home he toasted the health
Of a man who ne'er varied for places or wealth!

When supper was ended we spent all the night
In gay flowing bumpers and social delight;
With mirth and good humour did cheerfully sing,
"A health to John Arscott" and God save the King!

Hawker introduces the article by explaining that "Many a legend and record of his (Arscott's) times and deeds a century since, still float unembodied around the Oaks of old Tetcott.....". It is not clear whether he is the author of the ballad or is recounting oral tradition and in all likelihood, it was a combination of both. Hawker was a mystic, immersed in the stories and folk traditions of North Cornwall and there is sometimes a very fine line between his creative work and his retelling of oral tradition. He was also quite mischievous and allowed his own compositions to be passed on as traditional. For example, when he first published "Trelawny" in 1826 he allowed it to be seen as a traditional Cornish Ballad and did not admit authorship for several years. The fact remains that Hawker helped to boost the journey of "The Pencarrow Hunt" and if he did pen these words then he was perpetuating local legend in doing so.

By the time that Rev Sabine Baring Gould started his folk song collecting project in 1889 the ballad had become firmly attached to a tune and collected a "fol de rol" refrain. In the notes to the song published in Songs and Ballads of the

West [5] he makes no mention of Hawker but describes having found a great many variations of the ballad. The oldest he actually quotes a publication date for is 1880 [6], nearly 30 years later than Hawker's version. One of Baring Gould's sources apparently provided him with a partial copy of the song taken down by their mother circa 1820 but neither Baring Gould's notes in Songs and Ballads of the West nor his manuscripts[7] provide much detail. Following correspondence with the Game Keeper of Pencarrow, Frank Abbot, Baring Gould eventually attributed the origin of the ballad to one Dogget, a servant of the Arscotts who used to run with the hounds.

Baring Gould is quite disparaging of Dogget's version suggesting that he "spoilt and vulgarised" it from an older and finer ballad. This reveals more about Baring Gould than it does about the ballad. Baring Gould was caught up in the Romantic Movement of the time that saw folk songs as relics from a golden cultural past with a rich Bardic tradition. He also had a tendency to alter the songs he collected on publication to fit in with his view of what folk songs should be like and was not alone in this. Baring Gould gave concert parties to bring the songs he collected to a wider audience and, as "Arscott of Tetcott" included "The Pencarrow Hunt" in the programme, he was unhappy with the original text attributed to Dogget and changed the narrative so that that the hounds leaped off the cliffs at Penkenner closely followed John Arscott himself. Finishing with the verse:

---

[5] Sabine Baring-Gould, R. H. Fleetwood Shepherd, "Introduction", Songs and Ballads of the West: A Collection made from the mouths of the people, (London, Methuen & Co.1891).

[6] W.H.Luke. J.Arscott, esq of Tetcote and his jester Black John (Plymouth, W.H.Luke, Steam Printer to His Majesty, Bedford Street, 1880

[7] Baring Gould collection, Wren Trust available online at
https://www.vwml.org/record/SBG/3/1/11

When the tempest is howling, his horn you may hear,
And the bay of the hounds in their headlong career:
For Arscott of Tetcott loves hunting so well.
That he breaks for the pastime from Heaven – or Hell.

Baring Gould's biographers describe him as someone with a keen sense of the moral responsibilities of the landed gentry, and alcoholic hunting parties were probably not included in these responsibilities![8]

In terms of meanings and mediation it was the melody provided by the schoolmaster at Tetcott, J. Richards, which really inspired Baring Gould. He identified it with the Welsh tune "Difyrwch Gwyr Dyfi" from a collection of Welsh airs published by Edward Jones in 1784.[9] In his introduction to Songs and Ballads of the West published in 1891, Baring Gould suggests that Dartmoor and not the Tamar was the boundary between the Anglo Saxons of the East and the Celts of the west. He supports this by pointing out the distinctive nature of the melodies he found during his research in the area. A melody shared between the Celts of Wales and the Celts of the west fitted his world view perfectly. Several versions of the tune were identified by Baring Gould from oral tradition, but he felt that the modal variations provided by J. Benney of Menhenniot were particularly haunting and Celtic.

Cecil Sharp, who collaborated with Baring Gould to publish a revised edition of Songs of the West in 1905 had

---

[8] Holland Cohan Bickford Dickinson. Sabine Baring-Gould: Squarson, Writer and Folklorist, 1834-1924. (Newton Abbot, David & Charles, 1970), pp.117 and 123; See also Martin Graebe. As I walked out, Sabine Baring-Gould and the search for the Folk Songs of Devon and Cornwall, (Oxford, Signal Books, 2017)

[9] Edward Jones. Musical and Poetical Relicks of the Welsh Bards:Preserved by Tradition, and Authentic Manuscripts, from Remote Antiquity. (London: The author, 1784) p129

quite a different world view. Like Baring Gould he subscribed to the Romantic Movement and the notion of a past golden cultural age, but Sharp's was an English one and not Celtic! We find this reflected in the updated notes on the ballad in the revised edition. Here we find that the tune is now not Celtic at all but that it originates in England and is set to the Welsh words by Edward Jones. Notwithstanding the Celtic versus English debate, these various publications did serve to plough "The Pencarrow Hunt" / "Arscott of Tetcott" back into the domain of oral tradition.

The ballad was firmly reclaimed for the Celtic world by Celto-Cornish revivalist, Henry Jenner, when he submitted it for inclusion in Alfred Graves "Songs of the Six Celtic Nations" published in 1928.[10] Although this was after Baring Gould's death it had been planned for some time, Jenner had corresponded with him on the project and drew heavily upon his work for the Cornish section of this publication. The 1920s were a key period for the Celtic Revival in Cornwall and saw the formation of the Old Cornwall Societies and the inaugural ceremonies of Gorsedh Kernow. Folklore and tradition was an important element of the Celtic revival and "Songs of the Six Celtic Nations" ensured that ballads like "The Pencarrow Hunt" were included in the revival repertoire.

"The Pencarrow Hunt" makes quite a different appearance in the "Racca" project 1995-1997.[11] The aim of the project was to capture Cornish tunes in a moment of time from both oral tradition and contemporary composition. Two

---

[10] Alfred Percival Graves. The Celtic song book: being representative folk songs of the six Celtic nations. (London, E. Benn. 1928).

[11] Frances Bennet, Hilary Coleman, Nick Crowhurst, Merv Davey, Rosie Fierek, eds. Racca 2: Cornish Tunes for Cornish Sessions, (Calstock, Racca Project, 1997).

versions of the tune for "The Pencarrow Hunt" are included and are an expression of Cornish instrumental tradition. It is from here that the tune migrated to the Gwari Bosvenna, the Bodmin Play which takes place on the first Saturday in July as part of the Bodmin Heritage celebrations.[12]   Here the tune is used as the lament for the Beast when it is captured and found guilty of being Cornish.

The version of "The Pencarrow Hunt" provided here is its most recent apparition but one that echoes Baring Gould's ideas. Cornish folk musician, Richard Trethewy, was commissioned to provide an arrangement using a Cornish Language version of the words with the original Welsh tune by Lowender Peran Celtic Festival in November 2018 as part of its "Levow Brythonnek" / "Brythonic Voices" celebrations. No doubt "The Pencarrow Hunt" will continue its journey across the landscape and through time to bring us more stories and more insights.

You can see a video of Pencarrow Hunt, performed live by The Rowan Tree at Lowender Peran 2018 on our Facebook page. Search @LienGwerin

---

[12] Alex Langstone. From Granite to Sea: The Folklore of Bodmin Moor & East Cornwall, (London, Troy Books, 2018) p138.

Helgh Penkarow / Pencarrow Hunt

Y tardhas an jydh, ha'n myttin o splann,

Hag Arscott Tetcott ow seni y gorn

Ev a sonas mar ughel a-bervedh an chi,

An kebrow a grennas ha donsya dhe'n kri.

Y'n gegin an wesyon, y'n keunji an keun,

Y'n marghti an vergh a veu sordys gans an son,

Yskynna y vargh John Arscot a wrug,

Yn medh ev "Dewgh genev, a vebyon, war-rag!"

Y hwilsons y'n kelli, a Becket dhe Thorn,

'th esa Ringwood ha Rally, ha Princess ha Scorn,

Hag ena an lowarn a omdhiskwedhas dhe'n helgh,

a sewyas y eth, ow mos war y lergh.

Ha'n soper gorfennys, an nos spensyn ni

Owth eva dhe'n Myghtern ha'n ost meur y vri;

Y kensyn yn lowen gans levow fest gluw,

Yeghes da dhe John Arscott! Duw re sawyo an Ruw.

The daylight was dawning, right radiant the morn,

When Arscott of Tetcott he winded his horn

He blew such a flourish, so loud in the hall,

The rafters resounded and danced to the call.

In the kitchen the servants, in kennel the hounds,

In stable the horses were roused by the sounds,

On Black-cap in saddle sat Arscott, "Today

I will show you good sport lads. Hark! Follow, away!"

They tried in the coppice, from Becket to Thorn,

There were Ringwood and Rally, and Princess and Scorn,

Then out bounded Reynard , away they all went,

With the wind in their tails, on a beautiful scent.

When supper was ended we spent all the night

In gay flowing bumpers and social delight;

With mirth and good humour did cheerfully sing,

A health to John Arscott! And God save the King!

The Folklore Podcast Big Record project is now underway. The Big Record aims to restore the ethos of getting out into the field and recording our heritage before it is lost forever. Please contact Mark Norman by email for more information and how to take part. *thefolklorepodcast@gmail.com*

The Darley Oak

Rev. H. A. Simcoe

with additional notes by Alex Langstone

Giant of olden time!
Here in thy strength sublime,
A thousand winters thou hast brav'd the blast;
Thine ancient brethren gone -
Thou reignest here alone,
Last lonely remnant of the mighty past
Yet doth the voice of Spring
Old recollections bring,
Waking up buds and blossoms as of yore;
While 'neath thy furrow'd rind
Sweet influences wind,
And thou dost struggle to be green once more.
Scenes of a by-gone day
Now o'er my fancy play;
Strange eyes are on me – it is hallow'd ground: -
Priests strip the bending boughs,
They wreath their sacred brows,
And Druid worshippers are gath'ring round.
'Long Sharptor's granite mass,
Dark figures onward pass;

The wild is peopled – shouts are heard from far -
Adown the moory waste
Crowds with the victim haste,
And sacrifices smoke on bold Kilmar.
Past is the reverie;
And thou old hermit Tree
Art smiling calmly in the sun-set blaze:
Thus on my aged head
May God's own light be shed;
And my last effort be to shew his praise.

The Darley Oak near Linkinhorne, is suggested to be at least 1,000 years old and has been revered for centuries. Local folk tradition gives magical healing properties to the tree. It is said that any wish made by it will come true, and the trees acorns are said to be used as lucky charms, particularly giving luck to pregnant women. In particular anyone who passes through the hollow of the tree and then encircles the trunk will be granted any wish or desire. The tree was first documented as a tree of great antiquity in the 18th century and has been seen as a natural curiosity for generations. The present farmhouse was built in 1733; but the tree was revered well before this time. In the Eighteenth century, records show that the hollow in the trunk was *capable of housing small pleasure parties[13]*. The custom of holding tea parties in the Oak's hollow trunk was continued well into the 1980s by the Hoare family, who purchased the farm in 1919. [14]

[13] William Harvey, The Parish of Linkinhorne, 1727

[14] Alex Langstone. From Granite to Sea: The Folklore of Bodmin Moor & East Cornwall, (London, Troy Books, 2018)

Anima Mundi:
The Mysterious Carvings of Probus

Alan M. Kent

In 2004 my co-writer Danny L. J. Merrifield and I assembled a popular history of the mid-Cornwall parish and village of Probus[15]. In that volume we gave a history of the formation of the settlement and its surrounds, including an extensive consideration of the circular *Lann* [holy site] enclosure in which the Church of St Probus and St Grace stands. The present basic church building was constructed some time before 1530 and this was also the period in which the spectacular church tower (purported to be the highest in Cornwall) was constructed. During successive centuries there have been many alterations and changes to the building, most notably in the Victorian period. However, the outer

---

[15] Alan M. Kent and Danny L. J. Merrifield, *The Book of Probus: Cornwall's Garden Parish*, Tiverton: Halsgrove, 2004, pp.159-76.

superstructure has remained more or less constant over the five centuries since its construction.

The stone work of many parts of the church is quite impressive, but most notably a set of intricate quatrefoil carvings are found on the plinth of the base of the tower. Although now lichen and moss-covered, these are as impressive as other carvings on church architecture in Cornwall; notably the Church of St Mary Magdalene at Launceston.[16] The tower is also famous for a community in-joke which satirises Nicholas Carminnow, a local quarry owner, who supplied the stone. Carminnow apparently was slow to provide the masons with sufficient stone, and so as to mock him they carved a fox (the Carminnow family emblem) being chased by a dog. The carving of the fox and the dog can still be seen at the top of the plinth of the tower on the northern side of the church.[17]

Also visible in the church tower are three niches, which clearly one held long lost wooden statues, perhaps carvings of St Probus, and St Grace,[18] as well as possibly either the image of the Virgin Mary or Christ himself. Although these were destroyed in the Reformation, it is still possible to see a surviving fragment of wood inside the vestry, purported to have come from these icons. In the past, the overall effect must have been quite spectacular because the carved icons would need to have been reasonably large, as well as being gilded and very colourful. The tower itself was made of white granite, so given its height it must have shone like a beacon across the landscape.

---

[16] See A. G. Peter, *The Church of St Mary Magdalene, Launceston*, Launceston: The British Publishing Co., 1935.

[17] Kent and Merrifield, op.cit., p.167.

[18] Robert Hunt, *Popular Romances of the West of England: The Drolls, Traditions, and Superstitions of Old Cornwall (First Series)*, London: John Camden Hotton, 1865, p.277.

Although ignored by Merrifield and myself in the history of the parish, records of some mysterious carvings have since been discovered,[19] held in the Bodleian Library at Oxford, which correlate with a set of blocks of stone found on the southern edge of the eastern side of the church, specifically located close to the chest tomb of Sir Christopher Hawkins. The carvings are obscure, and at first glance blend in with the surrounding stone work. However, on closer examination the carvings appear to be highly distinctive. Some theories about their inclusion into the eastern side of the church may be considered here. One paradigm is that they were from another structure, possibly an earlier Medieval version of the church, and upon the remodeling were simply randomly incorporated into the new stone work. This would seem to be a logical recycling of resources. Whilst this may have been the case, the symbolic value of the carvings may have held a more mystical purpose, and they may well have been explicitly integrated into this end of the building since this is where the altar is placed. This would make sense since the altar itself is the holiest part of the church. In Probus this may have had added symbolic value since in a wall of the chancel is a reliquary in which the skulls of St Probus and St Grace are kept. Thus, if the carvings had symbolic importance this is reflected in their proximity both to the altar and to the founders of the church.

The carvings have somewhat faded and eroded away over the centuries, but they were certainly clear enough for the antiquarian Edward Lhuyd to observe, when he passed through Probus sometime in 1700. Lhuyd (1660-1709), as Williams notes, was a Welsh naturalist, botanist, linguist, geographer and antiquary.[20] He was in Cornwall in 1700 to record the

---

[19] Rawlinson D997 fol. 9v. The Rawlinson D997 manuscript is found in the Bodleian Library, Oxford.

[20] Derek R. Williams, *Edward Lhuyd 1660-1709: A Shropshire Welshman*, Oswestry: Oswestry Civic Society, 2008.

Cornish language in use and to collect its literature,[21] and indeed, his work has been instrumental in allowing scholars to observe and understand this phase of the language,[22] much of which has been crucial in determining the modern revitalization of this tongue.[23] Lhuyd was actually born in Shropshire, but from his family, he had a clear understanding of Welsh, and used this to commence comparative studies of Cornish, Breton, Manx, Irish and Scots Gaelic. The main focus of his work in Cornwall was in the West of the territory, but he was keen on mapping any antiquity of interest as he passed through, and hence his discovery of the carvings at Probus. He wrote the following in his notes about the carvings:

Crosses. Halfe circles, & other strainge figures on probus ye east south sid wall of Probus Church (on ye outside with an HIS in ye midstand these letters raised on ye one side ANMA ANIMA q. an Anima.[24]

The note is puzzling. It is still possible to identity crosses (some of which appear to be smaller 'Celtic'-style crosses, and the half circles are still discernable. According to the light and time of day, some carvings appear to represent figures, but this is by no means clear. The HIS referred to (and which is still visible) is probably IHS: a long held Christian

[21] Derek R. Williams, *Prying Into Every Hole and Corner: Edward Lhuyd in Cornwall in 1700*, Redruth: Dyllansow Truran, 1993.

[22] Alan M. Kent, *The Literature of Cornwall: Continuity, Identity, Difference 1000-2000*, Bristol: Redcliffe, 2000, pp.81-93; Brian Murdoch, *Cornish Literature*, Cambridge: D. S. Brewer, 1993, pp.131-4.

[23] Diarmuid Ó Néil (ed.), *Rebuilding the Celtic Languages: Reversing Language Shift In the Celtic Countries*, Talybont: Y Lolfa, 2005.

[24] Rawlinson, op.cit.

monogram, or more accurately a Christogram. This is a symbol often found adoring vestments. On the stone, because of the design, it would appear the letters may be read in various ways and this may account for Lhuyd's different version.

The Anma and Anima lettering is trickier to explain. In Jungian psychology the Anima is the 'inner self', though the carvings would clearly be too early for any interpretation of this kind.[25] Carl Jung was, however drawing on an earlier idea, this being the concept of *Anima Mundi*.[26] This is a Latin tern, sometimes meaning 'the soul of the world'. It defines the intrinsic connection between all living things on the planet, which importantly (as we are dealing with a Christian concept) relates to our world in much the same way as the soul is connected to the human body. The term appears to have had its origins in Classical philosophy, although we know that the concept had spread to the Atlantic periphery of Europe by the early Medieval period.

A contemporary analogy may even be drawn from George Lucas' *Star Wars* Jedi mythology, where 'the force' is conceived of in the same way. It could be that other letters are missing and that the blocks were once part of a longer sequence of writing now lost. Could that have originally read *Mundi* [the world]? We know that *Mundi* was a concept fully in the mind of the Cornish by the middle of the fifteenth century, since at Glasney College in Penryn, a scholar there wrote the title of one part of a trilogy of plays known as *Ordinalia* as *Origo Mundi*, which effectively translates to 'The Beginning of the World'.[27] The clergy at Probus would have

---

[25] Carl Jung, *The Psychology of the Unconscious*, Tel-Aviv: Dvir Co., Ltd, 1973 [1917].

[26] See David *Fideler, Restoring the Soul of the World: Our Living Bond With Nature's Intelligence,* Rochester, Vermont: *Inner Traditions, 2014.*

[27] *Alan M. Kent (ed. and tr.), Ordinalia: The Cornish Mystery Play Cycle, London: Francis Boutle Publishers, 2005.*

certainly had long-established connections to Glasney. It was indeed where many of them had trained. The connections are further reinforced by the fact that at Sorn Field, near to Trewithen (close by to Probus) there was once a Medieval amphitheatre known as a *plen-an-gwarry* (a 'playing place'), which likely hosted plays of a similar nature.[28] If such a play followed the format of other dramas in Medieval Cornwall, then the drama would have been an origin story of the local deities/saints, so here, we may conceive of a two-day, play perhaps based on the lives of St Probus and St Grace.

The 'q.an' is difficult to interpret as well. It may have course, just have been a short-hand term used by Lhuyd himself. Therefore, the carvings remain a puzzle. It could also well be that there are other such carvings embedded in the fabric of the church's exterior walls, but if they are high up, they would clearly be more difficult to see and interpret. A different kind of stone was used for the probable slightly later construction of the tower, so if the pieces were earlier, they were not integrated there. To the left of the present set of carvings, is substantial plant growth, which may, in fact, hide more carvings, but at present, it is impossible to discern their presence. The surviving set of carvings remains highly unusual though, and it would be interesting to hear from other readers of their own interpretations of their meaning and significance.

---

[28] *See Rod Lyon, Cornwall's Playing Places, Nancegollan: Taves an Weryn, pp.78-9.*

The Seaton Mermaid

Back in the days of Lyonesse, a little port throve on a fertile and wooded strip of coast which stretched where the waves break now, between Looe and the Rame, and a Mermaid who haunted its near-by caves lived in shy friendship with its fisher folk. Then one day some manner less youths among them waved the tail of a fish at her. Her fury blazed like a forest fire. No stick nor stone of the port escaped her curses, so that the creeping sands and seeping tides claimed all.

Teflon Tracey and the
New-age Squire

Andy Norfolk

It had mostly been a quiet week in St Bucca[29] when people first started noticing Tracey. Nothing more than the usual number of fights in the pub, but of course it wasn't feast day.[30] The maids had been couranting and courseying[31] after the boys as usual. It's funny how they maids manage to look like young goddesses when they're standing about chewing gum by the church steps. Of course, we all know that as soon as they get home butter wouldn't melt in their innocent little mouths. Meanwhile the lads try to impress them but end up acting like complete idiots, and when they get home – well they're still complete idiots.

Tracey was one of the gang of girls though you wouldn't have noticed her at first. Her adoptive mother didn't seem to think she was quite as important as gin and fags, so Tracy looked very dowdy until she got old enough to earn some money of her own. It was only really after the great stink in the village that anyone began to wonder about her. Mind you, they began to say afterwards that somehow the world had always seemed a bit brighter when she was around

---

[29] The original traditional story of "Duffy and the Devil" is based in St Buryan. The Bucca is a sort of nature spirit.

[30] Feast days are an annual event in many Cornish villages and fights have been a traditional part of the "fun".

[31] Couranting and courseying - well you can guess - used in "Duffy and the Devil".

and then there was what she'd managed to do with her mother's garden – always a picture that was.

Anyway, the village kids have been teasing old George for years about – well – his one remaining tooth and his legs which are so bent he couldn't stop a pig in an alley which accounts for the way he walks – sort of like he's drunk, but more rolling. Then they pinched some of his apples. Now they've always had a few and that's a normal part of village life, but this time they got organised. Strange that they don't remember from one year to the next that George grows cider apples which aren't worth eating. It seems it was the final straw when they stole that dump truck from the road works and filled it up, not that they managed to get it out of his orchard. George got his revenge, but he's always claimed his hand must have just slipped when he was passing the school bus queue in his muck-spreader. Though some of the village mothers was madder than wet hens at the extra washing, George wasn't so unhappy about it all in the end. He said down the pub that it'd saved him a lot of work picking up all they little apples and since somehow no-one thought to mention to Cormac[32] where their dumper was to, he got that as well.

And of course, that's when she started being called Teflon Tracey. Somehow, she was the only one who got missed by the great splatters of the smelliest muck George had been able to find – and that's when people began to say there was something – well not exactly strange – but anyway unusual about her. And some of the older folk gave each other knowing looks.

---

[32] Cormac is the Cornwall Council contracting business.

That anyone should think she was a bit different was odd in itself, because St Bucca is a bit unusual. It's always had an "atmosphere" all of its own. Practically every other family has always been full of more charmers and pellars[33] than you could shake a stick at. Not that you'd want to, in case they shook one back. Emmets arrive by mistake and see it in Summer, believe the estate agents when they say St Bucca has a unique character, which it does, buy one of the houses to stay but leave after a few months, muttering stuff about deliverance[34]. There was a film crew came here once wanting to make some film or other – wicker dogs or some such[35] - anyway the crew stayed just one night before deciding to go somewhere less weird. I reckon their mistake was to ask if they had any special local real ale in the pub. That's the Queens Head, but it was built at Bucca's Bottom, so that's what everyone calls it. The landlord is a bit of a herbalist and home-brew specialist and you don't get anything much more real than his henbane beer.

'Not long after George's revenge someone did move into the village and stayed, at least for a while, which the locals reckoned was a sign that he was really odd. He arrived having sold a big house up country for a fortune and came to Cornwall to find a new life. He said he'd been called. The locals were damned sure they hadn't invited him, but then he was a gift-horse like any other vurriner. So, they were always please to see him in the pub to hear about his latest bit of foolishness, especially as he also seemed to believe everything he was told about local ways, which was some fun. But then, as they say

---

[33] Pellar means sort of white witch and healer.

[34] Deliverance the film - but you probably got that.

[35] They made "Straw Dogs" in St Buryan

locally, you always get the truth straight from the "Bucca's Bottom". And it was reckoned a good thing that he seemed to have a very short memory about who'd bought the last round. He'd bought the old Rectory, which was reckoned to be another good thing in the village. Thing is that it was a ramshackle old place built as a proper job back in Victorian times. Now we all know what a proper job is. Yes it's a job you do just well enough to last for a while but which will need a bit more doing in a few months so you keep on earning. Well the rectory had been kept up proper-job style for years and was a sure source of lots of work.

When he first moved in he kept asking about committees, said he wanted to do his bit for the community. Well he soon found out that he wasn't going to get any say in running things, but he still kept trying to take things over. Course that's when he first started getting called Squire. Interfering busybody thought it was a sign of respect. Then he had some sort of funny turn. The village reckoned he'd been drinking more of that well water than he should. He started getting into that spirituality, kept going down that library in St Just where they've got all those funny books to[36]. After he'd read each one he told everyone that he'd finally found what he'd been looking for – again and again! And he got into what he called being more open and expressing his feelings. Anyway, he got very expressive in the pub one night and started telling everyone he loved them. Some fun more that was. Anyhow that's when he became known as Squire Love-all[37].

---

[36] Cheryl Straffon who was a librarian at St Just was one of the Cornish Earth Mysteries committee with me - was responsible for St Just library having some odd books.

[37] The original story includes Squire Lovell.

He discovered that their water divining and went wandering about with a couple of coat-hangers on the ends of bits of string. All very mystical he reckoned – kept muttering about his son and a servant![38] Well of course the village thought this was hilarious. "What's he want they old bits of wire for then", they said down the Bottom, the pub that is. "They lines is everywhere. Any fool can feel they". A couple of the old boys added to the fun by moving the lines around a bit once he reckoned he'd dowsed a place completely. He got mazed as a brush with it all, but the final straw was when they wound a couple of the lines together. His coat-hangers spun round so fast the strings wrapped round his neck and nearly strangled 'en. He decided he'd better try something else, though he said it was because he'd mastered dowsing!

Next up was shamanism. Some stuff about loving animals in a spiritual way. Well they soon told him straight down the pub that he'd better keep it spiritual. But all that happened was he was seen out in his garden and at they old stones banging a little drum with a dachshund with its legs tied in knots painted[39] on it and moaning to himself and then singing a bit of the song the cat died with. "Tidn' much fun then, this shamanism?" they asked in the pub. He said he was trying to get into a trance state, so they bought him a Henbane special. Seems he wasn't ready for a proper trance after all, but it didn't take too long to clean up. They reckoned he had plenty to moan about anyway living in that big, old, draughty, damp house on his own, eating that rabbit food and without a

---

[38] There's a book about dowsing energy lines across Britain by a couple of local authors called "The Sun & the Serpent"

[39] Many shamans use drums with animals painted on them often with Celtic knotwork patterns.

telly. And that jumped-up Council wouldn't even have let him put in some nice draught-free plastic double-glazing. P'raps that had something to do with why his friends didn't seem to want to visit more than once.

Then there was the time he got into Druidry – not that proper stuff they do up the Gorsedh, but some funny stuff dressing up in white sheets with bare feet. Of course, he went off that soon enough after a couple of downpours at dawn – nearly caught his death of a chill and spent weeks picking bramble spines out of his toes. About then was when the village finally decided he must be a didgan[40] deaf and too slow to carry cold dinner. See he asked in the Bottom about local history. They told him about the old Queen's Golden Jubilee and how George's great-grand-faither Arthur put on a grand tableau with knights and all and about Arthur's wife Pen who was a bit of a dragon. Then they told him about how Arthur shot the stuffed chough[41] they've got in the bar and how they reckon there's a bit of the old devil in it cos of the way it leers and winks at unsuspecting emmets. Next thing Squire Love-all's going round saying that St Bucca must have been the original everlong with lots of camels or some such.

He says apples were important back then – maybe that's what they fed all they camels? So, he reckoned he had to plant an orchard of his own. Now it was a bit daft to ask old George for help – he didn't want no competition for his cider and apple brandy business – but he gave the Squire a few

---

[40] "Didgan" = a little bit.

[41] They've got a stuffed chough in the pub in St Buryan and there's a legend that Arthur lives on as a chough or raven on the cliffs of Cornwall.

seedlings from his hedges. No chance they'd grow into anything worth having he thought and anyway the Squire seemed to have purple thumbs. First lot all died. Second lot didn't. Squire saw Tracey's mum's garden and asked Tracey to help. She talked to every tree as she planted it – in the right sort of spot – and watered them and looked after them. George was mazed and horrified when they grew to six foot in a year and blossomed the next spring and set a heavy crop. And those in the village who knew about these things nodded to each other and were extra nice to Tracey. "Proper little Bucca she be!" they said.

Then it seemed Squire's money was getting a bit thin. Less trips to the Bottom and less asking others to fix things at the Rectory. So the next thing is, he says down the pub, he'd better make some cider and can George help? Well George couldn't wait to help – to make sure he had no chance of making anything worth drinking. Sure enough he turned out some stuff that was so sour and vinegary that no one would drink it. George said it must be something wrong with his soil but seeing as how he'd helped he'd take it off his hands to use instead of creosote. Funny how about then George bought a lot of marmite and molasses and then sold a lot of stuff to that Stein bloke up Padstow – he called it Bucca's Tears Cornish balsamic vinegar.

When the cider didn't work out Squire seemed to really be between the hardwood and the driftwood. So he says in the pub now he's learnt all these psychic and spiritual skills, like how to get dolphins into channels or some such, he thought he ought to share his wisdom... He reckons he needs to start running courses for rich people so that they can become shamans and dowsers and druids and all too. Over just a couple of days – so as he can share his skills with more people. This is when the village starts thinking he might fit in after all.

First off, he advertises all fancy – weekend retreats with renowned wisdom master in authentic Celtic setting, personal tuition in the secrets of the ancients, £10 each. Well no-one wants to know – so he asks down the Bottom what he's doing wrong. Course it's obvious to one and all – so he advertises at £1000 each and soon gets lots of bookings. Trouble is it still doesn't quite work and there's mutterings about Trades Descriptions Acts. He carries on and gets Tracey to help for a bit of local colour. Turns out that Tracey's good at that there guru stuff. She sends people into proper deep trances where they really meet their ancestors – scared some of 'em witless. And healing – well she only had to wave a finger towards someone and they was good as new. The piskies didn't just talk in squeaky voices to they punters[42], they pinched em black and blue as well. Very experiential that was. And her workshops on Celtic Shaman Tantric Feng Shui were legendary. She even did all the cooking – and made Squire's rabbit food taste like it was worth eating, but then she added real rabbit. So, all of a sudden word spreads and Squire's little enterprise becomes very popular and he starts to get a few more proper jobs done at his Celtic Reawakening and Programming Centre – though he changes the name after what the villagers start calling it. Still they're quite proud of him in a way – this sort of stuff that he's doing is a proper job and no mistake! People keep coming back to learn the next stage of the path to becoming a realised master like him.

---

[42] One local character used to run courses at a large house near Lamorna and took people into his fogou, talking in squeaky voices pretending to be the piskies.

Then disaster strikes. Though she'd moved into the Rectory, Tracey had been keeping her own life and more important staying out of Squire's. Anyhow his problem really started back with George's revenge because Tracey was rather impressed by one lad who was better at looking a complete idiot even when covered in muck than the rest. Now it all took some time to happen, but eventually she and Huey Lanyon[43] got to going out. Huey being a local boy soon spotted the rather large flaw in Tracey working for the Squire, which was that she did all the work, dealt with all the punters and the he took almost all the money. So Huey and Tracey decide they'll set up their own New-age centre and make a nice living off gullible folk from up country. Now Squire's sick as a gurnet because he knows he can't run things without Tracey. Then the damned fool gets drunk and stands there sweating like a poultice and ups and asks her to marry him. Tracey isn't impressed and Huey's all for giving him a good larruping. Tracey says she'll show him how to run things properly – a sort of course in the secrets of the ancients from a renowned wisdom master – and it needn't take more than a weekend. Oh and she'd only charge him £1500 as a special rate for one-to-one tuition.

Of course, she doesn't stop helping out all at once because he starts paying her a lot more. Still he tries running workshops on his own... but it doesn't quite work. He'd just run a disastrous course on crystal healing in which he slipped and embedded his best selenite[44] wand into someone's bum – nearly the last straw and he comes over all queer and has to be

---

[43] Huey Lenine is Duffy's boy-friend in the original story

[44] Selenite is a clear calcite crystal which is fairly easy to carve into wands - very trendy at the mo'.

looked after by the women on the course. They sat him down in the kitchen with a big mug of sweetened Bach remedy and a sandwich. Well the Squire took a big mouthful of the sandwich and chewed it with satisfaction – gradually giving way to a feeling of disquiet. "This is meat", he said accusingly. "Oh yes", said the woman who made it, "it's from my own Tamworth pigs". The squire spat it out on the stone just beyond the threshold where it landed in the little hollow he'd been told was for offerings to the piskies. "Piskies, you're welcome to it "he said and then went back into the kitchen sitting down with his hands over his eyes, feeling strangely light-headed. Now those of you interested in the Celts will realise that he'd just performed the ritual for finding things out known as Imbas Forosna.[45] So what happened? This voice in his ear said, "The real name gives power!" And he was so shocked at having a proper psychic experience that he fell off his chair.

He spends the next day nursing his bruises and thinking about this and reckons it must be about how to get Tracey to stay. Some of what he's read in all they books has seeped in somewhere and he knows names are powerful. Now she's adopted so no-one knows what her proper name might be.... Her stepmother just looks at his as if he's proper mazed when he asks her what Tracey's name is. Still he has an idea and starts to follow her around. She'd been going off dancing with a bunch of witches over Sancreed way. Seems they must have been catholic witches 'cos they were dancing some sort of rhythm method.[46] Anyhow she's also going to the old places

---

[45] Imbas forosna is a ritual described in old Irish texts which involves chewing the flesh of a red pig (or dog or cat), offering it to the spirits and going into a trance.

[46] Friends of mine some of whom are witches used to dance regularly in Sancreed to a "wave" of 5 rhythms.

with some of her friends and working with the land. Those in the know in the village give each other even more meaningful looks now. She's definitely one to look after – things start going better when she does this sort of stuff. Then on the 1st of February, which happens to be her birthday, she really gets into her stride at the Maidens[47]. Proper young goddess she is then, not that Squire quite sees it like that; mind he's halfway through a gorse bush at the time, prickled to death and freezing cold. He can more or less hear what's going on, though it somehow doesn't sound like proper English. Anyhow the others keep calling her Duffy, so he thinks, "That's it. I know her real name. Now I can make her stay".

So next day first chance he gets he calls her Duffy and tells her that now he knows her real name she'll have to stay. She soon finds out he's been sneaking round after her and just laughs at him. She says if he's going to try and do things like that she's moving out for good. So it's all up with Squire and he sells up soon as he can and moves off to some seaside town where he can be part of a community experiential workshops initiative.

Of course, if he'd bothered to learn any Cornish it could have turned out different. He could have had some handsome power then all right. What they were calling her was Dywvyrgh, that is God's girl – 'cos they knew she was the Bucca's daughter.

---

[47] Many local stone circles are called the Nine Maidens.

Cruel Coppinger

Sheridan James Lunt

In the West, it seems,
Traffic was widely condoned,
Where it is still sometimes said
No Cornish jury will convict a Smuggler.
And when a hundred men or more
Were needed to dispatch a run,
In a Country of villages
One and All must be party to the trade.

John Coppinger however
Was not so well thought of.
In truth such shameful things
Are told about the Man
That if believed
Unfolds a tale
Of the Devil's own left-tenant;
Wicked and corrupt beyond measure.

Spat from a failing Four-mast
In a dirty storm,
The Villain dragged himself dreckly
From the icy spume,
And with what remained of any strength
He leapt upon a Maiden's mount,
Galloping her stolen
Under the worried watch of the Powerless.

The poor girl he made his wife and hostage,
Putting her human frailty through carnal tortures
By which to extort all that was her due
In deeds and titles;
So making himself Lord at Hartland
And Master of that stretch.
From there he saw his racket;
Dilating a hateful sphere.

A more sinister cult
There never has been
On the brutal coast
That cut so many criminals.
Coppinger's gang was evil;
Raping innocents,

Maiming the weak.
Wreckers and Pirates to a Man.

With every Magistrate under the thumb,
Mobsters did how they pleased,
And any with wit kept well away
Lest they be stung, or worse;
When Good Boys disappeared:
Abducted for decks of the contraband fleet,
Some missing years without word to their Kin.
Others never came back.

Flush in health and all things,
With a distorted Son to succeed him,
Some wondered that Coppinger might never go.
The Dane cast a Mountain shadow on land and sea;
Making livelihood hard,
Making days seem dark.
But tides turn,
And Coppinger's luck was done.

Was it prayers answered
For the Parson he lashed with ninetails?
Did Piskies revenge the poor Tailor
Coppinger dragged from his charger?
His wife perhaps met a Witch
To close some contract with unnatural power?
The Man, on every side, had enemies enough,
Each swelling with glee at the worsening news of his defeat.

Trade sank in squalls;
Deckhands bailed;
The King's Cutters hung in the bay;
So that with sideways smirk

Coppinger tossed his goblet in the hearth
And swaggered out that night
To loose himself in the same salt waters
That kecked him up.

No mortal stood by to watch him drown.
Neither came no angel.
Only Satan
Would stalk the wretch;
Come at the moment
The last little bubble quit his lung.
Thus, concludes the life of Coppinger.
Remembered evermore as Cruel.

For more wonderful art and words see *Piski Tells the Cornish Legends* at piskifilms.wixsite.com/cornish-legends

Traditions of Parcurno

William Bottrell

A ghostly ship, with a ghostly crew,
In tempests she appears;
And before the gale, or against the gale,
She sails without a rag of sail;
Without a helmsman steers.
                                        Longfellow.

Not long since a general belief prevailed in the western parishes that in ancient times Parcurno was the principal port of Cornwall, and that, until the Cove became "sanded up" there was sufficient depth of water to float the largest ships then made, in to the foot of an old caunce (paved road) which may still be seen.

One old story ascribes the choking of Parcurno and Parchapel to the mischievous spirit Tregeagle, who was sent to Gwenvor Cove and there required to remain until he made a truss of sand - to be bound with ropes spun of the same - and carried it to a rock above high-water mark. For many years he toiled in vain at his task, and his howling would be heard for many miles away when winds or waves scattered the sand he had piled up during low water.

One very frosty night, however, by pouring water from Velan-Dreath brook over his truss he succeeded in making it hold together and bore it to a rock above the flow of spring tides.

Then, as some say, that very night, as he took his way over or along the coast towards Helston, to revisit and torment those who raised him from the grave, by way of showing his exultation at having completed his task, or for mere deviltry perhaps, he swept all the sand out of Nanjisel and around Pedn-pen-with into Parcurno and adjacent coves, without letting any enter Pargwartha.

Another tradition says that sweeping the sand from Nanjisel to the east of Tol-pedn was assigned to Tregeagle as a separate task. After this exploit the troublesome spirit was again sent to Gwenvor to make a truss of sand. There he remains toiling to this day - unable to perform what is required in order to regain his liberty, because he was bound not to use Velan-Dreath water or any other.

There is also a very old belief that spectre ships frequently visited Parcurno, both before and since its navigable channel became filled with sand, and that they were often seen sailing up and down the valley, over dry land the same as on the sea. These naval apparitions were, in olden times, regarded as "tokens" that enemies were about to make a descent; the number of phantom vessels foreboded the sea-robbers' approaching force.

This presage of yore was held for truth by many old folks but lately deceased; yet latterly it has somehow changed its character and become connected with the history of a person who, little more than a hundred years ago, lived in a lone house called Chygwidden, about a mile inland from Parcurno. This comparatively modern story also accounts for the sand shifting and has appropriated old traditions that had no connection therewith.

It relates that, long ago, Chygwidden was the chief dwelling-place of a family who flourished in St. Levan for a few generations and then all its branches became so reduced, through riotous living, as to be obliged to mortgage and sell much of their freehold lands.

The eldest and only son, by a former wife, of old Martin T——, who lived there, took to a seafaring life when about twenty, on account of cruel treatment received from his drunken father and a step-dame several years younger than himself. On leaving he vowed that he would never return whilst one lived who then darkened his father's doors.

Many years passed, and as no tidings had been received of young Martin, as he was still called, most persons believed him dead. In the meantime, his father, the step-dame, and her children, having all died within a few years of each other, a distant relative, as heir-at-law, had taken possession of what little property remained, and lived in Chygwidden.

Some ten years after the decease of all who had lived under old Martin's roof when his eldest son was driven thence, a large ship hove-to within a mile of Parcurno on a fine afternoon in harvest time. People working in fields near the cliff noticed the unusual circumstance and saw a boat leave the ship with two men, who landed in Parcurno with several chests and other goods, and the ship proceeded on her course.

It was evident that one of those who came on shore was well acquainted with the place, as he struck at once into a pathway over the cliff which led, by a short cut, to Rospeltha where he made himself known as young Martin T—— and procured horses and other help to take several heavy chests and bales to Chygwidden.

There was great rejoicing when it was known that the wanderer had at length returned to claim his own. His kinsfolks - a young man and his sister Eleanor, a damsel in her teens -were ready to resign possession, but Martin then cared little for house or land, and told them to keep the place and welcome, for all he desired was to have a home there for himself and his comrade whilst they remained, which he thought would only be for a short spell. His tastes had changed with change of scene. The place that he had once deemed the fairest on earth but then he had seen no more of it than was visible from the nearest high hill - now appeared dreary; and the people whom those of his own family excepted - he once thought the best in the world now seemed a forlorn set of consequential, grimly-religious nobodies to him, and above all to his mate, who, by-the-bye, requires more particular notice than we have yet bestowed on him.

Martin found the people, also, much altered from what they were in his youthful days, for about the time of his return a new sect had sprung up whose members, professing uncommon godliness, decried our ancient games and merry-makings, which were wont on holidays to unite all ages and classes. Their condemnation caused them to fall into disuse; and, on account of the censorious and intolerant spirit which then prevailed, there was much less heartiness and cordial intercourse amongst neighbours than formerly.

In a short time, however, Martin, now called by most persons "The Captain," became reconciled - one can't say attached - to his native place and the "humdrum West Country folks," as he styled them, who marvelled at his riches and the change which had taken place in his outward mien and manner. Yet the homely people's surprise at the alteration in

Martin was nothing to their wonder, allied to fear, excited by his dusky companion or slave, for no one knew in what relation they stood to each other.

This stranger was seen to be a robust man, about thirty years of age apparently, with a swarthy complexion, many shades darker than the Captain's Spanish-mahogany tinted skin. Martin called this man José or mate and he rarely spoke a word of English (though he could when he pleased) or addressed anyone but Martin, with whom he always conversed in some outlandish lingo which seemed more natural to the Captain than his mother tongue. A tantalizing mystery shrouded the dark "outlander" for his master or friend would never answer any queries respecting him. He was almost equally silent with regard to buccaneering or other adventures, and rarely spoke of anything that occurred either at home or abroad during his absence. The two strange beings often came to high words and even to blows, but they would never allow anyone to meddle in their quarrels. When Martin was drunk and off his guard he would now and then ease his mind by swearing at his mate in plain English, or grumble at him in the same, to the effect that he had risked his life and spent a fortune to save him from being hanged at the yard-arm. "Discontented devil of a blackamoor," he would say, "why canst thou not be satisfied to live here? Thou art bound to me body and soul; and do I not indulge thee with everything gold can purchase?"

José would sometimes murmur "Avast there; all our gold and diamonds can't procure us here the bright sunshine and joyous people, nor the rich fruits and wine, of my native clime."

He seldom, however, made other reply than by gloomy looks or fiery glances which soon recalled Martin to his senses. It was remarked that after these outbursts of passion he was for a long while like the humble slave of his mate.

The boat in which they landed was kept at Parcurno, except for short spells during stormy times of the year, when she was put into Penberth or Pargwartha for greater safety; and, weeks together, they would remain out at sea night and day till their provisions were used; then they would come in, their craft laden with fish, and this cargo was free to all-comers. Stormy weather seldom drove them to land; they seemed to delight in a tempest.

Before winter came, they procured a good number of hounds, and great part of the hunting season was passed by them in coursing over all parts of the West Country. Often of winter's nights, people far away would be frightened by hearing or seeing these two wild-looking hunters and their dogs' chasm over some lone moor, and they gave rise to many a story of Old Nick and his headless hounds.

When tired of the chase, weeks were often passed at a public-house in Buryan Church-town. Martin treated one and all and scattered gold around him like chaff. The tawny mate, however, at times restrained Martin's lavish expenditure, took charge of his money-chests, and refused him the keys.

José would occasionally condescend to express his wishes to Eleanor, who was mistress of the rare establishment. She understood and humoured the pair, who took pleasure in decking her in the richest stuffs and jewels that their chests contained or that money could procure, and she frequently stayed up alone best part of the night to await their return.

After being at home a year or so the Captain had a large half-decked boat built, and several rocks removed in Parcurno to make a safer place in which to moor her. They then took longer trips and were not seen in Chygwidden for months running. The two eccentric beings passed many years in this way and held but little intercourse with their neighbours.

At length Martin perceived tokens of death, or what he took for such, and made his man swear that when he saw signs of near dissolution, he would take him off to sea, let him die there, and send him to rest at the ocean's bottom. He also bound his kinsman by oath not to oppose his wishes and invoked a curse on anyone who would lay his dust beside the remains of those who had driven him to range the wide world like a vagabond.

They might have complied with his strange desires, but ere they could be carried out he died in a hammock, suspended in his bed-room.

Now there comes a mystery, that is not likely to be cleared up.

It was known that a coffin, followed by the cousins, José, and the dogs, was taken to St. Levan Churchyard and buried near the ground in which Martin's family lie. But it was rumoured that the coffin merely contained earth to make weight.

The following night, however, the dark "outlander" had two chests conveyed to Parcurno, the largest of which was said to contain the remains of his friend, and the other money and valuables which belonged to himself. The chests placed on board the half-decked vessel, José and his favourite dog embarked, waited for the tide to rise, and put to sea; but no one remained at the cove to behold their departure, and no more was seen in the West of man, dog, or boat.

Eleanor disappeared on the funeral night and it was believed that she left with the stranger, who was scarcely a league to sea ere a tempest arose and continued with great fury for nearly a week; and, although it was in winter, the sky of nights was all ablaze with lightning and the days as dark as nights. During this storm Parcurno was choked with sand, and no boat could be kept there since.

The tempest had scarcely lulled when an apparition of Martin's craft would drive into Parcurno against wind and tide; oft-times she came in the dusk of evening, and, without stopping at the Cove, took her course up over the old caunce towards Chapel-Curno; thence she sailed away, her keel just skimming the ground, or many yards above it, as she passed over hill and dale till she arrived at Chygwidden.

The barque was generally shrouded in mist, and one could rarely get a glimpse of her deck on which the shadowy figures of two men, a woman, and a dog, were beheld now and then. This ship of the dead, with her ghostly crew, hovered over the town-place a moment, then bore away to a croft on the farm, and vanished near a rock where a large sum of foreign coins was disinterred many years ago, so it is said. Of late the ghostly ship has not been known to have entered Parcurno, and on account of innovations recently effected, there she may nevermore be seen in that ancient port.

Some North Cornwall Folklore

Alex Langstone

The full moon rides high in the starry sky above the Camel Estuary. Silver shadows are cast across the flood plains and salt marsh where the river Amble flows into the wide mouth of the crooked river. Standing on the bank below the old bridge is a solitary figure. Staring across the marsh towards the softly illuminated hills he stands, silently waiting. It is close to midnight, and he nervously watches the old road from Wadebridge. Owls screech at one another from the nearby trees, and the gentle trickle of the river breaks the sweet silence of a Cornish night.

The faint sound of hooves clattering on the road emerges from the silver landscape, slowly becoming louder. The watching figure moves towards the road, anticipating what might manifest from the moonlight. Then the rumble of cart wheels is heard and the crack of a coachman's whip. Then at once all becomes clear. A shimmering apparition of a gleaming coach pulled by two black horses' rattles across the historic bridge. However, as soon as it reaches the opposite bank of the river it suddenly and mysteriously disappears, as if it was never there. And all is silent once more, save for the soft sounds of the flowing river and the nightly conversation of the owls.

The eighteenth-century crossing of Trewornan Bridge is the scene of the above tale, where a ghoulish coach and horses is said to appear, when the moon is full. Trewornan Bridge is the obvious 'gateway' to this small yet mysterious North Cornwall peninsula that gives rise to many legends, mysteries and folklore. The peninsula is formed by the Camel estuary in the south and west, and by the wild coastline of the Celtic Sea in the north. The central area pivots upon the parish of St Minver and it was Nicholas Roscarrock who recorded the following 17th century folktale from this remote district.

One fine day, whilst St Menefrida was combing her hair by her ancient chapel and holy well at Tredrizzick, she was rudely confronted by the Devil, who appeared from the deep shadows of the local woods. She was so distressed by his astonishing apparition, that she threw her comb at him, striking the fiend with such force that he flew through the air and plunged into the ground at Topalundy, on the nearby coast. This created the great hole, now known as Lundy Hole, sited high on the clifftop above Lundy Cove, close to Polzeath. This vast collapsed sea cave is a spectacular and inspiring site, both from the clifftop and the beach. It sits like a giant 'landscape hag stone', casting a protective arm across the cove.

On a broad sweeping bend at the tidal edge of St Minver Lowlands is an area known as Gentle Jane. The name has been linked with the riverside field since at least the early nineteenth century and it has been suggested that it was named after a local eccentric *'Gentle Jane'*, who has been vaguely recalled in local oral traditions as an outsider and recluse, who healed the sick and helped those in need. Rumoured to be an expert herbalist, she lived by the estuary in seclusion, close to where the remains of Wheal Sisters copper mine stand. Here she made herself available to help all those in need, including the pirates operating along this stretch of coast, who knew that she was a safe refuge when illness and accident threatened.

Not far from Gentle Jane, hidden in the centre of a sprawling golf course lies Jesus well. This lovely holy well on the dunes at St Minver may be linked to the nearby church of St Enodoc, who according to Nicholas Orme had his feast on the first Wednesday of March each year. Robert Charles Hope recorded some lore from this well in his book: *The Legendary Lore of the Holy Wells of England (1893)*.

The spring was visited by children suffering from whopping-cough, Quiller-Couch adding that children were dipped in the water. Quiller-Couch also tells us that:

People came from long distances to pay their devotions and use the waters, which were celebrated for many cures, and for the evils which befell scoffing unbelievers. Its virtues continued till late years. No longer ago than 1867, Mary Cranwell.... who for a considerable period had suffered severely from a skin disorder, and could obtain no relief from medical treatment, fully believing, as she stated to the author, from the repute of the well, that if she bathed in the water with faith she would be cured of her disease, went to the place, and kneeling beside the well recited the Litany to the Holy Name of Jesus, and bathed the diseased parts in the waters. She received relief from the first application; and repeating it the prescribed number of three times, at intervals; she became perfectly whole, and has never since suffered from the same malady.

Thomas Quiller Couch was recording tales around Polperro and eastern Cornwall around the same time as Bottrell was collecting folklore in the west, and he recorded a strange custom where:

At some wells a cross of rushes or straw is floated on the surface of the water, to sink or swim as Fate decides. Coins were also left on a niche in the well, or cast into its waters as an offering; this custom seems to have entirely disappeared in Cornwall at least, although at one well, Jesus Well, St. Minver, it was a distinctly remembered practice: it was probably a much older custom than the dropping in of pins; for setting aside the fact that pins were not in use until the sixteenth century, there is never any mention in the old accounts of the skewers of wood or bone of former days being among the offerings to the naiad.

Jesus well's folkloric origins are from an unknown Celtic saint, (possibly St Enodoc or St Petroc), who whilst travelling the area, became thirsty and struck his staff into the ground. The water bubbled up miraculously and the saint could drink.

In her introduction to her volume entitled The Piskey Purse, Cornish folklorist Enys Tregarthen hints at some old lore from the cliffs around Polzeath and district. Where the piskey folk, (often referred to as 'the little ancient people' around North Cornwall) inhabited the cliff tops and hidden coombes.

"The spot most favoured by the Piskeys for dancing was
Pentire Glaze cliffs, where, alas! Half a dozen lodging-houses
now stand. But the marks of fairy feet are not, they say, all
obliterated, and the rings where Piskeys danced may yet be
seen on the great headland of Pentire, and tiny paths called
'Piskey Walks' are still there on the edge of some of the cliffs."

In the middle years of the nineteenth century an old woman called Mollie W. lived in an ancient tumbledown cottage at the historic Pilchard fishing village of Port Quin. She was often described as "an evil woman". One day her neighbour's pigs accidentally crossed her doorstep. In temper, she pronounced that they should never cross Port Quin Bridge alive again. The poor pigs had their sty on the other side of the bridge and within a few hours of them returning home, they died. Rumours quickly spread that the pigs had been bewitched by Mollie. The old woman used to ill-wish the cattle belonging to a local farmer (Mr. T), and to break the spell, Mrs. T (who must have been skilled in the arts of a Charmer) used to burn the heart of a dead animal, pierced with pins. This was placed on the fire at Midnight, after which the cattle stopped getting ill and dying. Mollie always used to visit Mrs. T the day after, as after the heart burning charm the witch must speak to the person she has wronged before she is at peace again. There is an old legend attached to Port Quin. The pilchard fishing industry had been a prosperous one up until around 1840, when it started to go into decline. As a result, the village dwindled to the size of a hamlet and its demise gave rise to the local legend of disaster at sea. It states that one Sunday, breaking the Sabbath, all the fishermen of the village put to sea but were lost in a great storm that destroyed the entire pilchard fleet.

A curious old tradition about the old Washing Pool of Port Issac was recalled in the Winter 1951 Old Cornwall Journal by Norma E. Lovell, who states that when her father was young (around 1900) there was an old spring at Port Issac known as the washing pool. This spring was known to possess healing properties and was situated in a field on a cliff overlooking the harbour. In the past, the folk of the village used to wash their clothes at this spring, and they would spread them out to dry in the field. During times of drought the spring water was collected as it cascaded over the cliff edge. One of the old cures from this spring was recorded as

"By being pressed face-downwards across the stream three times, children were believed to be cured of whooping cough. Other streams which ran from north to south were often credited with similar healing properties."

Port Isaac also has its very own sea-serpent. In 1935 a monstrous glossy black creature was spotted in the sea. It was reported to have a long goose-like neck, a humped back and a tremendous tail. This sea-serpent was seen by several witnesses and one of them, a local postman was keen to stress that he was a teetotaller.

Local farmers at Port Isaac used to perform a Corn-dressing charm to protect their crops from being owl-blasted (cursed). The method used was as follows. The seed was mixed with copper sulphate by turning it with a shovel three times. Once turned the top of the heap was marked with a cross using the handle of the shovel, then in each quarter of the cross a horseshoe was drawn. This charm was still in use in the 1940s in and around the district and here we have a fascinating glimpse into the farming folklore on the north coast from the first half of the twentieth century.

On the opposite side of the small peninsula lies he Iron Age fort of Castle Killibury, otherwise known as Kelly Rounds. The site dates to between 400 and 100 BC, and measures about 230 metres in diameter and is flanked by ramparts and ditches and has an entrance to the east. Legend states it to be King Arthur's Court of Kelliwic. Excavations have revealed evidence of occupation of Castle Killibury from the Bronze Age through to the Iron Age.

Nearby lies the site of King Arthur's god-daughter, Endelyn. The old saint is also known as Endelienta, and she has many legends surrounding her. She is linked to cattle and kept a cow at her hermitage at Trentinney, where she lived as a hermit. Legend says that she subsisted solely on the milk of her cow, and the water from two nearby wells. Her sister, St Dilic or according to Roscarrock, St Ilick or St Telick, settled nearby and the two would often meet along a certain path whose grass would always grow greener than elsewhere. There was a holy tree linked to St Dilic, which sat by her holy well, and a curse lay upon anyone who dared to damage the tree.

One story tells us that St Endelyn's cow was killed by a neighbour when it strayed onto his land, and Endelyn's Godfather (said to have been King Arthur) then killed the neighbour in retaliation. Endelyn was mortified by these acts of violence and miraculously brought both the cow and the neighbour back to life. Legend also states that Endelyn asked a cow to find her final resting place by pulling her body on a wooden sledge. Where the cow stopped, she would be buried.

The 15th century church, which lies to the north of Trentinney, is thought to be the spot that the cow chose for her, and she was buried here shortly after her death, which in folklore is said to have occurred close to May Day, sometime during the mid-6th century. Her old church is well worth a visit, as it contains the remains of the stone base of her medieval shrine, along with a very beautiful modern icon of the saint painted by John Coleman. It is a truly peaceful and sacred building containing an air of mystery and sanctity. There were two ancient holy wells nearby where legend states that Endelyn herself used to visit and just a mile to the north is the 6th century Brychan stone. This cross was removed during the 19th century, and placed on the headland at Doyden, where it suffered very bad erosion. Thankfully it was returned to its original site in 1932 by Bodmin 'Old Cornwall' Society.

For loads more on the folklore of Bodmin Moor and eastern Cornwall, please see my book *From Granite to Sea.* Available direct from the publisher's website at *www.troybooks.co.uk* or if you prefer, I have a few signed copies available direct from me from my own website *www.alexlangstone.com*

The Battle of Vellan-Druchar – A Real Event?

Craig Weatherhill

Both Robert Hunt and William Bottrell tell of this little-known Arthurian battle in the Land's End peninsula of Cornwall. In short, the legend tells of the landing of "Sea Kings" or Danes landing their ships at Gwenver, near Sennen Cove, working their way inland and across the isthmus of Penwith to the vicinity of the Hayle estuary, looting and pillaging as they went, before turning back.

But, from the moment they landed, the beacon fires of alarm had been lit, a whole series of them shining out from one hilltop to the next until the blaze a thousand feet up on Condolden Hill was seen by Arthur's retinue at Tintagel. Arthur (always "Prince Arthur" in the West Cornish legends) led a force under nine chieftains down through the length of Cornwall and met with the invaders at Vellan-druchar, a valley site one mile east of St Buryan.

The slaughter was terrible, with every last man of the Danish force being wiped out by the Celtic force and the carnage was so great that the millwheel downstream was worked by "Danish mix'd with Cornish blood", rather than by water. The Celtic force then made for Gwenver, where other Danes had been left to guard the ships, but other forces were at work against the invaders.

A local wise-woman wove a spell to raise a west wind by sweeping the church from door to altar and emptying the holy well against the hill. The elements obliged, the strong westerly gale coinciding with a spring high tide to drive the ships high onto the beach where they lay stranded. The guarding force was helpless as Arthur's forces swept down on them to kill every last man. The ships lay where they were for years until they rotted away. Arthur and the nine Cornish chieftains gathered for a victory feast at the tabular rock called Table-maen, which still exists at Mayon near Sennen, whereupon Merlin made an appearance to intone one of his customarily gloomy prophecies foretelling the end of the world should the millwheel ever again be turned by a flow of "Danish mix'd with Cornish blood".

Could this legend be a folk-memory of real events? Clearly, as a late 5th or early 6th century Arthur is featured, the date is far too early for Danes ever to have been involved. They showed no interest in Britain until they raided Lindisfarne in 793, and when they did turn up in Cornwall, in the 9th century, the Cornish formed an alliance with them against their common foe, the West Saxons.

If the invading enemy of the legend was not the Danes, then might these marauders instead have been Saxons, whose homeland lay at the base of the Danish peninsula? At first glance, this seems unfeasible, as no Saxon foot, other than priestly ones, is known to have touched Cornish soil until the 9th century at the very earliest, but another alternative is well worth consideration.

During the mid-5th century, Saxon pirate ships led by a man named Corsold had made their way down the Channel and established a base on islands in the estuary of the Loire river in Gaul. From here, they made a thorough nuisance of themselves in the Bay of Biscay. By the late 460s, Corsold had been succeeded by the formidable Odovacar who cast inland and took control of the town of *Andegavum* (Angers). This was a threat too far, and in 469 or 470, an alliance of Gallo-Romans, Franks and a detachment of Britons retook *Andegavum* and cleared out the pirate bases. Odovacar, no mean opponent, got away, and set out on other ventures that led to him becoming the first Germanic king of Rome in 476.

Things went badly after that in the disintegrating Roman province of Gaul. The army under the British king's leadership, all 12,000 of them, took up a vanguard position near Chateauroux and Bourges, was betrayed to Euric, king of the Visigoths, in Aquitaine, by Arvandus, Prefect of Gaul and Deputy Western Emperor, who had ambitions of his own. While temporarily isolated from the Gallo-Roman army, the Britons were decimated in a surprise attack by Euric. The king and other British survivors managed to withdraw into neutral Burgundy where they disappeared from historical record near a town named Avallon. (And if this sounds remarkably familiar, it IS real and recorded history that a certain Geoffrey of Monmouth surely used in his fanciful c.1136 account of King Arthur!). Childeric of the Franks turned on the Gallo-Romans in 486 and killed their leader Syagrius, turning Gaul into the land of the Franks: France.

With all this turmoil going on in Gaul, the surviving Saxons had the chance to rebuild their pirate base at the Loire estuary and resume their nefarious activities as the scourge of the Atlantic seaways. A Visigothic admiral was to complain about forever being on the lookout for the "curved ships of the Saxons".

Then, in 471, Irish annals record a "second Saxon raid on Ireland" (record of the first and its date do not seem to have survived), and here a likely scenario for the Battle of Vellandruchar begins to take shape.

That seafaring Saxon raiders would sail all the way from the North Sea coasts of their homeland to raid Ireland, at that early a date, is entirely unlikely, and by far their most convenient point of departure would surely have been their established pirate base in the Loire. Once their ships had rounded Ushant, the journey would have been managed in two stages, for jutting out right in between Ushant and Ireland is the "halfway house" of the Penwith peninsula of Cornwall, poorly defended and ripe for the plucking.

So, the landing of a Saxon fleet on a safe beach near to Land's End in the latter half of the 5th century is a wholly feasible proposition in historical terms, and there is little evidence that West Penwith was, at that time, at all well defended. Chûn Castle may have been re-occupied at that time, but indications are that its post-Roman garrison was more concerned with the tin trade and protection of the major transportation route of the metal, from its extraction and processing locations to the ports on St Ives Bay and Mount's Bay, rather than the defence of the peninsula.

The port at St Michael's Mount was probably manned by a small defence force to protect its commercial value, and the Mount was equipped with Iron Age cliff castle defence lines, but the remote beach at Gwenver would be completely vulnerable and unguarded – a perfect landing spot for an invading force. The population of the area primarily consisted of farmers and tinners who could not be expected to offer any meaningful resistance to several shiploads of ruthless warrior-pirates, and they would have been far more likely to make a run for the hills. All that was practically available for local protection was the beacon system that the legend is careful to detail and emphasise.

The possibility of a Saxon incursion into West Penwith from the sea in the late 5th century is, therefore, realistic, but what of the Cornish force that came in response to the alarm beacons?

The legend states that Arthur led a force commanded by nine chieftains, that is, consisting of nine divisions. Cornwall, at that time, was divided into six *keverangow*, areas that could each provide a fighting force and later known as "Hundreds". The word *keverang* has cognates in Welsh (*cyfrang*) and Middle Breton (*cuuranc*), the latter meaning a military assembly. The Cornish *keverangow* appear to be been run on similar lines to the divisions of the Welsh kingdoms called *cantrefi* ("100 settlements"), which had administrations and courts of their own, headed by major landowners known in Welsh as *uchelwyr* (Cornish: *ughelwer*), "high men, nobility" and which were also expected to provide a war host when required by the regional High King; in Cornwall's case, the King of Dumnonia.

The number nine seems excessive and does not gell with the six *keverangow* that then existed, even though they later became nine. It is quite possible that the number represents a magical exaggeration. Three is a magically powerful number in Celtic lore; 'three times three' triples its mystic power. If this was the case, then the number of military divisions that actually departed from Tintagel might, in reality, have been just three, and this leads to another curious coincidence. Tintagel is located in the *keverang* of Trigg, its modern name a contraction of *Trigor*, "three war hosts"; the name being recorded as *pagus Tricurius* in the 7th century, and *Tricorscire* in King Alfred's Will c.881. Interestingly, it was later, c.1200, sub-divided into three "Hundreds": Trigg, Lesnewth and Stratton but, from its name, could provide three fighting forces well before that.

The legend could, therefore, be reconstructed in this way in order to achieve a feasibly realistic scenario:

A fleet of Saxon pirates set out from the Loire on a bid to raid Ireland. They stop off at the halfway point of the Land's End peninsula, landing on the remote beach of Gwenver, and, meeting with no resistance, mount a major raid on the area that takes them as far as the Hayle estuary, and probably spans a period of three or four days.

The chain of alarm beacons reaches Tintagel in less than an hour, alerting the King of Dumnonia's garrison which, in turn, summons the cavalry forces of the three war hosts of the Trigg *keverang*. Under the overall leadership of, not Arthur, but the Dumnonian king himself, probably Tudwal or maybe Kenvawr at this time, they make way at speed down through the length of Cornwall.

By the time the Cornish forces reach West Penwith, the Saxon raiding force, consisting solely of foot-soldiers, are already on the return journey toward their ships, and are caught up with at the valley location of Vellan-druchar. The Cornish cavalry outflank, surround, and overwhelm them, wiping them out in a terrible slaughter before moving further westward to mop up any further Saxon warriors at the landing place at Gwenver, where foul weather and a high spring tide has stranded their ships. No invader is left alive, Cornish casualties are probably light, and the invaders' ships are either burned or left to rot.

The Dumnonian king and the three divisional commanders give thanks for the victory at the nearby *carrek sans*, or holy rock, of Table-maen before resting and making their way back to North Cornwall.

In later years, the locally unprecedented event lasts long into folk memory and, as time passes, becomes written into the Arthurian cycle of myth.

Within sight of Gwenver, and a mile and a half off Land's End itself, is the long and dangerous reef known as the Longships, now marked by a lighthouse on what was once its tallest crag, its line of several fearsome rocks projecting well above high water mark. From where did the reef get its unusual name? That this is an old name is confirmed by a record dated to as long ago as 1347, naming the reef as *Langeships*. Might this also have stemmed from folk memory, as bearing a fanciful resemblance to the procession of Saxon longboats that had once sailed past Land's End from the south, ominously heading into Gwenver?

Above: J. T. Blight's 19ᵗʰ century illustration of Table-maen

Author Notes and References

The Pencarrow Hunt by Merv Davey.

Merv Davey comes from a family rooted in Cornish folk tradition. His great grandmother used to play for dances on the fish cellars at Newquay in the 1880s and his grandfather was a step dancer. Merv has been involved in a variety of Cornish folk bands and dance groups over the years and helped to research the music and dance for these groups. A spell in a pipe band in the 1980s confirmed a passion for bagpipes which he has since transferred to the medieval variety including the Cornish pipes. In 2005 he undertook postgraduate research at Exeter University's Institute of Cornish Studies and was awarded a PhD for his thesis. Merv was elected Grand Bard of Gorsedh Kernow in 2015 and alongside of this role he took the story of Cornish folk tradition (and bagpipes) as far as Australia. He continues to work with the family group, North Cornwall Ceili Band, and together with his wife Alison travels far and wide as itinerant piper and drummer.

The Darley Oak by Rev. H. A. Simcoe.

Taken from *The Light from the West, Vol. 1*. Published in 1834. Simcoe lived at Penheale near Egloskerry and was curate of the village from 1822 to 1846. Simcoe wrote and published many books on antiquarian subjects, produced from his own printing press at Penheale. He died at the manor house on 15 November 1868 and was buried in the village churchyard.

The Mysterious Carvings of Probus by Alan M. Kent.

Alan M. Kent was born in Cornwall and graduated from the Universities of Cardiff and Exeter, specialising in Celtic and Anglo-Celtic literatures. He is Senior Lecturer in Literature for the Open University in South-West Britain and is a Visiting Fellow in Celtic Studies at the University of La Coruña, Galicia. His novel Dan Daddow's Cornish Comicalities won the Holyer an Gof Prize for Fiction in 2018. His latest book is *The Festivals of Cornwall: Ritual, Revival, Re-invention* (2018). His stage adaptation of The Mousehole Cat (based on the folklore of Tom Bawcock's Eve will tour internationally in 2019.

The Seaton Mermaid.

From the Old Looe Stories and Legends set of cards (1937) Author and artist unknown.

Teflon Tracey and the New-age Squire by Andy Norfolk

Andy Norfolk is among other things a writer, illustrator, dowser and Bard of the Cornish Gorsedh. He has had many interesting and odd experiences at ancient sites, including having a long conversation with a spriggan on Zennor Hill and hearing the hummadruz there too. He was one of the founders of the Cornish Earth Mysteries Group. He's had a life-long interest in folklore, partly thanks to Falmouth library in the 50s and 60s, and has written assorted articles about it. He wrote a series of stories for the old CEMG Yule gatherings based on local sites and with a nod to Cornish folk tales. Teflon Tracy is one of those, imagining how Robert Hunt's story of Duffy and the Devil might be told now.

Cruel Coppinger by Sheridan James Lunt.

Sheridan James Lunt learnt to draw and paint in the 1990's at the St. Ives School of Painting and went on to study the fine arts at Falmouth College of Arts. He founded his independent film company Piski Films in 2009 and began animating the Cornish Legends in 2014. The series 'Piski Tells the Cornish Legends', which now retells five classic stories, can be seen on youtube, and in 2019 the work of presenting the short films in the Cornish language was begun in partnership with Kowethas: the Cornish Language Fellowship. An illustrated book is also available on the website: http://piskifilms.wixsite.com/cornish-legends

Traditions of Parcurno by William Bottrell

Originally published in Bottrell's Traditions and Hearthside Stories of West Cornwall, Vol. 2, 1873.

Some North Cornwall Folklore by Alex Langstone

Folkloric musings about a favourite corner of Cornwall from your editor, who is also the author of *From Granite to Sea: The Folklore of Bodmin Moor and East Cornwall* and *Menhir: A poetic invocation of the Cornish landscape.*

The Battle of Vellan-Druchar by Craig Weatherhill.

Craig Weatherhill, writer, archaeologist, historian, folklorist and Cornish language expert. He is a bard of Gorsedh Kernow and lives in West Cornwall. His most recent books include *The Promontory People; An Early History of the Cornish* and *They Shall Land; The Spanish Raid on Mounts Bay, Cornwall, July 1595.* His fictional *Lyonesse Stone Trilogy* contains a wealth of legend and folklore from the Penwith peninsula.